WONDERS
OF THE
USA

Carron Brown

Illustrated by Bee Johnson

A DIVISION OF EDC PUBLISHING

The United States of America
is a land filled with wonders.

Explore its caves and rivers,
visit its national parks and view
its historic buildings.

Shine a flashlight behind the page
or hold it to the light to reveal
the amazing sights in and around
our country. Discover a land
of great surprises.

In a classroom, children are learning about the United States.

What do you think the teacher is showing them?

It's a map of the United States.

There are a lot of amazing things to see in the 50 states that make up our country.

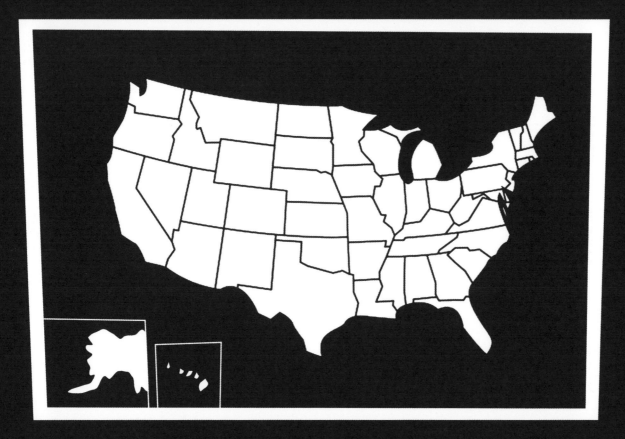

The White House, in Washington, DC, is home to the President of the United States.

What is happening in the White House today?

There are important
meetings here.

Ssh!

Listen!

People from all around the world visit the
White House to speak with the president.

The faces of four presidents are carved into Mount Rushmore in South Dakota.

Who is looking at them?

Many people come to see Mount Rushmore.

Almost three million tourists
visit every year.

Click!

The huge Statue of Liberty stands on an island in New York Harbor.

Can you see inside her crown?

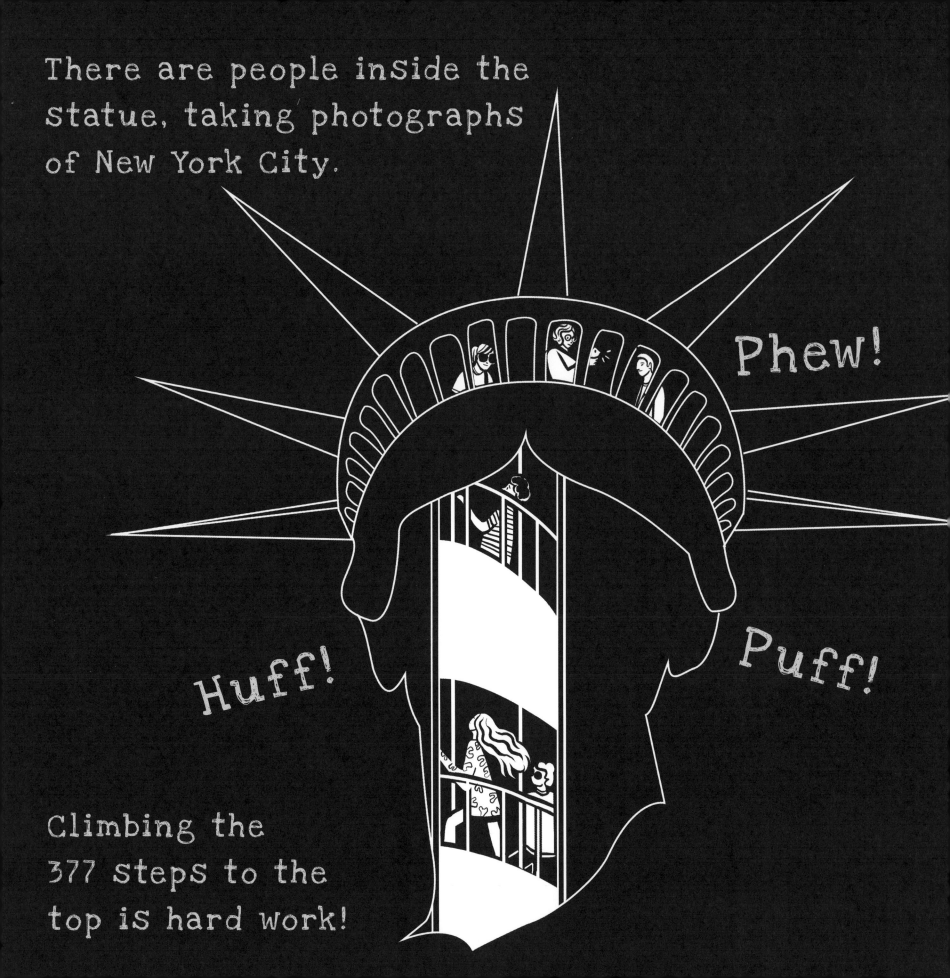

These people have been visiting Independence Hall in Philadelphia, Pennsylvania. The Declaration of Independence was signed here.

What are they looking at now?

They are looking at the Liberty Bell.

The bell is old and very famous.
Can you see the large crack?

It's time to dress up for the Mardi Gras festival in New Orleans, Louisiana.

Everyone wears bright colors and costumes. Can you see some butterfly wings?

This little girl is dressed up as a butterfly!

People ride on colorful floats and throw beads into the crowd as they pass through the city.

NASA's Mission Control Center in Houston, Texas, is an exciting place. From here, scientists help astronauts on space missions!

What are these flight controllers looking at?

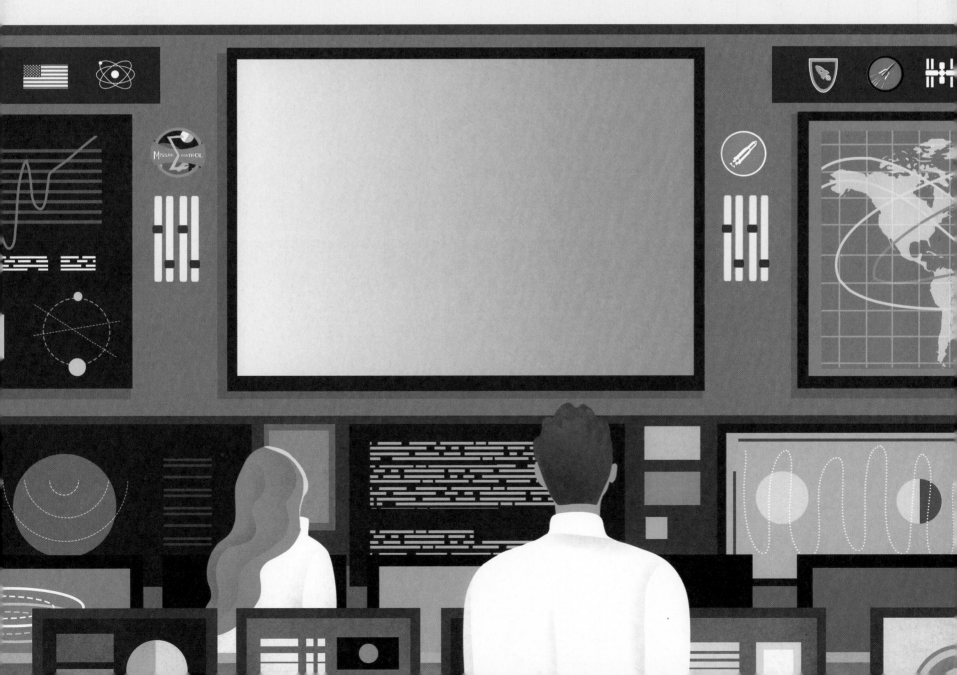

They are watching a rocket
taking off into outer space.

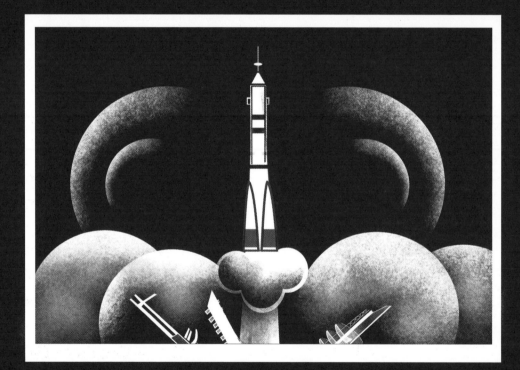

Blastoff!

A thick fog fills the air in
San Francisco, California.

What are these orange towers attached to?

The Golden Gate Bridge!

The bridge is painted orange so that ships can see it in the fog. It also has horns that toot loudly to warn boats that the bridge is near.

Stretch!

Grand Canyon National Park is in Arizona.

Over many years, the Colorado River carved a deep, steep canyon into the rocks.

Can you see any animals?

There are two ground
squirrels behind the rocks.

Many kinds of animals live in the
canyon's trees, rocks and river.

Squeak!

scuttle!

The highest mountain in the country is Denali. It is in Alaska.

Who is heading toward the mountain?

A group of hikers.

They are wearing warm clothes
and are carrying backpacks
filled with food for their hike.

The Everglades is a vast wetland in Southern Florida.

People explore the area by boat.

What is lurking in the water?

It's an alligator!

These dark-gray reptiles hold their
breath when they are underwater.

Flaps cover their ears and nose
So water can't get in.

snap!

The most famous cave in New Mexico is Carlsbad Cavern. Long stalactites hang from the ceiling.

What is sleeping in the cave?

zzzzzzz!

Around 400,000 Brazilian
free-tailed bats sleep in
the cave during the day.

At night, they fly
out of the cave
to eat insects.

This heated pool of water, called the Grand Prismatic Spring, bubbles and steams in Yellowstone National Park in Wyoming.

What's behind the trees?

There are four bison eating grass.

Bison are the largest animals in Yellowstone National Park. They roam in groups called herds.

Grunt!

The state of Hawaii is a group of islands.
The beaches here are beautiful.

Can you see a surfer?

Here he is!

People travel to Hawaii to
surf the enormous waves.

The bald eagle is our country's national bird.
It can be seen in many different states, as far
north as Alaska and as far south as Florida.

Where is this bald eagle flying to?

Her nest! She has two chicks to feed.

Cheep!

Cheep!

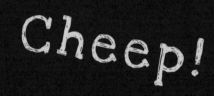

The American flag is called the Stars and Stripes. It has 50 stars—one for each state.

We live in a great country filled with many wonders!

There's more...

Did you enjoy your whistle-stop tour of the United States?
Here are more facts about the famous sights you have seen.

 **White House** This awesome building has 132 rooms and was once the biggest house in the country. The president's family lives in the center.

Mount Rushmore It took around 400 people 14 years to carve the heads of presidents Washington, Jefferson, T. Roosevelt and Lincoln into Mount Rushmore.

 **Statue of Liberty** This gigantic figure represents freedom. It was a gift from France, made in 1886. It was sent in pieces on a ship and rebuilt in New York City.

Liberty Bell The Liberty Bell used to hang in the tower of Independence Hall. It was made more than 250 years ago.

 **Mardi Gras** A King and Queen of Carnival are chosen each year. Their floats are the most colorful.

Mission Control The flight controller at each desk looks after a different part of a mission, from liftoff to communication.

Golden Gate Bridge
Every year, around ten million tourists visit this world-famous bridge. It stretches almost 1.7 miles across San Francisco Bay.

Grand Canyon
This canyon is huge! It is 277 miles long, over 1 mile deep and 18 miles wide.

Denali
The top half of this mountain is always covered in freezing-cold snow and ice. The name "Denali" means "The Great One."

Everglades
All kinds of wild animals live in this national park. It's the only place in the world that is home to both alligators and crocodiles.

Carlsbad Cavern
This cavern is one of more than 100 underground caves. They formed in the time of the dinosaurs, when sea would have covered this land.

Yellowstone
This was the world's first national park. It is located on top of a supervolcano!

Hawaii
This is the only state that is made up of islands. There are eight main islands and more than 100 smaller ones.

Bald Eagle
This bird doesn't actually have a bald head. Its head is covered in white feathers.

First American Edition 2017
Kane Miller, A Division of EDC Publishing

Copyright © 2017 Ivy Kids (an imprint of Ivy Press Ltd)

Published by arrangement with Ivy Press Limited, United Kingdom.

For information contact:
Kane Miller, A Division of EDC Publishing
PO Box 470663
Tulsa, OK 74147-0663
www.kanemiller.com
www.edcpub.com
www.usbornebooksandmore.com

Library of Congress Control Number: 2016934254

Printed in China

ISBN: 978-1-61067-543-7